EASY VIOLIN REPERTOIF

with simple piano accompaniment

Short **Violin** Pieces

Arranged by Hywel Davies

Bosworth

(a division of Music Sales Limited)

8/9 Frith Street, London W1D 3JB, Great Britain.

Exclusive distributors:
Music Sales Limited
Newmarket Road, Bury St. Edmunds, Suffolk IP33 3YB, England.

Order No. BOE005179
ISBN 0-7119-9642-3
This book © Copyright 2003 Bosworth.

Compilation by Jeremy Birchall.
Additional fingering and bowing by Hywel Jenkins.
Music Engraved by Andrew Shiels.
Cover designed by Michael Bell Design.
Printed in Great Britain.

Your Guarantee of Quality:
As publishers, we strive to produce every book to the highest commercial standards.
This book has been freshly engraved and avoids awkward page turns making playing from it a real pleasure.
Particular care has been given to specifying acid-free, neutral-sized paper made from
pulps which have not been elemental chlorine bleached.
The pulp is from farmed sustainable forests and was produced with special regard for the environment.
Throughout, the printing and binding have been planned to ensure a sturdy,
attractive publication which should give years of enjoyment.
If your copy fails to meet our high standards, please inform us and we will gladly replace it.

www.musicsales.com

Anything Goes

Words & Music by Cole Porter

Autumn

from 'The Four Seasons' No.3, 1st movement

By Antonio Vivaldi

Barcarolle
from 'The Tales of Hoffmann'

By Jacques Offenbach

Can-can

from 'Orpheus in the Underworld'

By Jacques Offenbach

Can't Take My Eyes Off You

Words & Music by Bob Crewe & Bob Gaudio

Chanson de Matin

Op.15, No.2

By Edward Elgar

Dam Busters' March

By Eric Coates

Ding Dong Merrily On High

Traditional

E.T. The Extra Terrestrial

By John Williams

Fly Me To The Moon (In Other Words)

Words & Music by Bart Howard

Frosty The Snowman

Words & Music by Steve Nelson & Jack Rollins

Intermezzo

from 'Cavalleria Rusticana'

By Pietro Mascagni

I Have A Dream

Words & Music by Benny Andersson & Björn Ulvaeus

Jean de Florette (Theme)

By Jean-Claude Petit

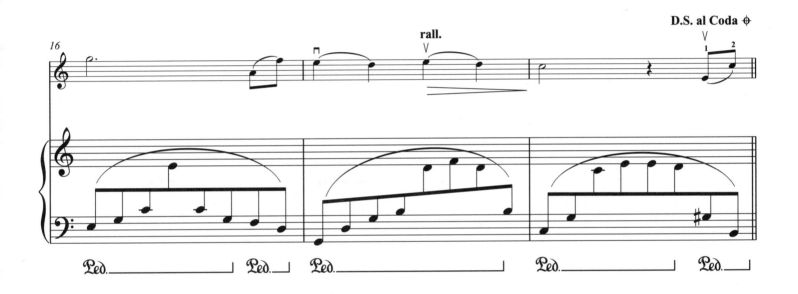

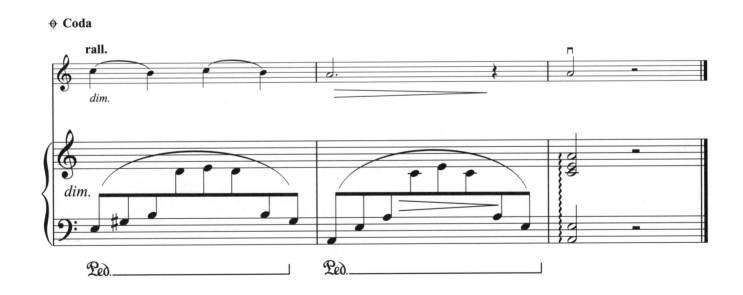

Jeeves And Wooster

Music by Anne Dudley

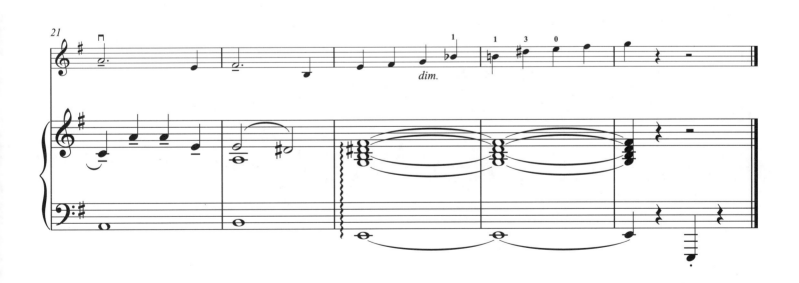

Jingle Bells

Words & Music by J.S. Pierpont

Music To Watch Girls By

Words & Music by Anthony Velona & Sidney Ramin

Nobody Does It Better

from the movie 'The Spy Who Loved Me'

Words by Carole Bayer Sager
Music by Marvin Hamlisch

Queen Of My Heart

Words & Music by John McLaughlin, Steve Robson,
Steve Mac & Wayne Hector

Schindler's List

from the movie 'Schindler's List'

By John Williams

Silent Night

Words by Joseph Mohr
Music by Franz Gruber

She's The One

Words & Music by Karl Wallinger

Smoke Gets In Your Eyes

Words by Otto Harbach
Music by Jerome Kern

Spring

from 'The Four Seasons' No.1, 1st movement

By Antonio Vivaldi

Yesterday

Words & Music by John Lennon & Paul McCartney

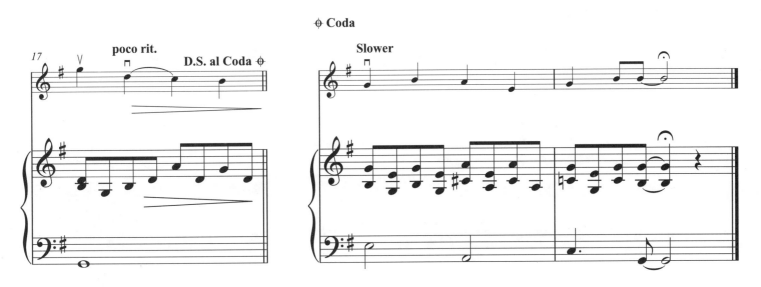

You've Got A Friend In Me

from the movie 'Toy Story'

Music & Lyrics by Randy Newman

39

Theme from 'The New World' Symphony

Symphony No.9 in E minor Op.95

By Antonin Dvorak